De Grazia

AND MEXICAN COOKERY

Art by TED DE GRAZIA

Recipes by RITA DAVENPORT

REVISED

NORTHLAND PUBLISHING

Front cover artwork and De Grazia photo
Courtesy of De Grazia Gallery in the Sun, Tucson, Arizona

www.northlandpub.com

First Edition
Ninth Printing, 2004
ISBN 0-87358-307-8
Library of Congress Catalog Card Number 82-80299
Printed in China

CONTENTS

PREFACE

Two extraordinary art forms greeted me when I moved to the Southwest in 1968: Mexican food and the works of De Grazia. I quickly acquired an affinity for the vibrancy, texture, and flavor of both.

As a home economist, I soon learned more about the nuances of Mexican cookery. To discover more about the man behind the artwork, I traveled to Tucson to meet De Grazia.

I was just starting out in broadcasting and had found that famous people could be very intimidating. Not De Grazia! His gentle, easy manner helped me relax. A psychic who was visiting his gallery that day noted the easy rapport between De Grazia and me and commented that we were possibly father and daughter in another lifetime. I don't know about that, but I did feel as if we had known each other before.

De Grazia's early years were ones of great struggle, contributing perhaps to the compelling contradictions which mark his present life style. He is possessed of both a warm, caring spirit and a compulsive need for privacy.

It is through his art that De Grazia shares with the world his generosity, sensitivity, and love.

He and I have been friends now for a decade and we continue to grow closer. Even when I am not around this talented human being I can sense him in his paintings, which reflect back to me the love I feel toward him. I wish the world knew him as I have been blessed to know him. In ten years of broadcasting I have had a chance to interview many famous people. He is truly the most impressive.

This cookbook combines his love for art with my love for cooking.

APPETIZERS

CHALUPAS

These little boats are delicious topped with a small dollop of sour cream and a slice of radish or ripe olive.

2½ cups masa harina
¼ cup all-purpose flour
1 teaspoon salt
¼ teaspoon baking powder
¼ cup melted lard or shortening
1 egg, beaten
1 cup lukewarm water
cooking oil for frying

In mixing bowl combine masa harina, flour, salt, and baking powder. In separate bowl, combine shortening, egg, and water. Add to dry ingredients and work with hands until dough is well mixed and holds its shape. Cover and chill. For each Chalupa, pat about 2 tablespoons of the dough into an oval-shaped cake about 3–4 inches long. Pinch edge with fingers to form a ridge. Heat ½-inch cooking oil in skillet to 365 degrees. Place Chalupa in hot fat with ridge down. Cook for 30 seconds; turn and cook until golden and

crisp on other side. Remove from skillet and drain on paper towels. Fill each with meat mixture and top with grated cheese.

FILLING:

> ½ pound ground beef or chorizo (removed from casings)
> 1 tablespoon cooking oil
> ½ cup chopped onion
> 1 large tomato, peeled and chopped
> 1 4-ounce can chopped green chilies
> ½ cup shredded longhorn Cheddar or grated Romano cheese

Brown ground beef in oil. Drain off excess fat. Add onion, tomato, and chilies. Mix well.

YIELD: 30 Chalupas

CHILI-CHEESE BALL

Cheeses and chilies may be combined ahead of time for a spicy treat served with chips or crackers.

> 2 cups grated sharp Cheddar cheese
> 1 3-ounce package cream cheese, softened
> ½ teaspoon garlic powder
> 1 teaspoon Worcestershire sauce
> ¼ cup diced green chilies
> chili powder

In a small bowl combine cheeses, garlic powder, Worcestershire sauce, and green chilies; mix well. Shape into a ball, pressing firmly between palms of hands. Roll in chili powder until well coated. Serve as an hors d'ouevre with corn chips or crackers.

Note: Roll cheese ball in finely chopped parsley or chopped nuts if chili powder is too spicy for personal taste.

YIELD: 1 cheese ball

CHEESE CRISP

Everyone's favorite appetizer, just waiting for a choice of garnish.

flour tortilla
longhorn Cheddar cheese, grated

Warm large flour tortilla by placing on an ungreased, heated griddle or frying pan. Turn once. Sprinkle with a generous amount of grated cheese. Allow to cook until cheese melts and becomes bubbly. Remove to warmed serving dish, garnish with favorite topping or serve plain. Cut into wedges with sharp knife or utility scissors.

The flour tortilla may also be sprinkled with grated cheese and placed under broiler until cheese is melted. When prepared this way, the tortilla is not as crisp.

Note: Cheese crisps are great topped with guacamole, salsa, or bean dip. They become the "Mexican Pizza" if topped with chopped green onion, chopped tomatoes, diced green chilies, or cooked chorizo sausage.

SOPES

Sopes may be cooked ahead of time and assembled just before serving. Having a little salsa nearby for guests to spoon on top is a good idea.

- 2 cups masa harina
- 1 teaspoon salt
- ¼ cup all-purpose flour
- 1 cup lukewarm water
- 1 egg, beaten
- ¼ cup melted lard or shortening
  cooking oil for deep fat frying
- 2 tablespoons butter or margarine
- ½ cup minced onion
- 1 medium tomato, peeled and diced
- 1½ cups refried beans
- 1 cup shredded longhorn Cheddar cheese
  sliced radishes, sliced olives, or canned
  green chili slivers

In mixing bowl combine masa harina, salt, and flour. Stir in water and egg. Add lard or shortening; mix well. Work dough with hands until it will hold its shape. Chill if necessary for easy handling. For each sope base, shape 1–2 tablespoons of the dough into a ball and pat into a flat round cake, 2–2½ inches in diameter. Fry in deep fat (365 degrees) until golden. Remove and drain on paper towels. Melt butter or margarine in a small skillet over medium heat. Add onion; sauté until tender. Stir in tomato; remove from heat. Meanwhile, top each sope with 2 teaspoons refried beans, about 2 teaspoons onion and tomato mixture, and about 1 teaspoon shredded cheese. Place on an ungreased baking sheet, heat in a 400 degree oven until cheese starts to melt. Remove from oven and top with radish slice, olive slice, green chili.

YIELD: Approximately 30

NACHOS

A Mexican hors d'oeuvre favorite, may be topped with diced green chilies for those who prefer them hot.

½ cup refried beans, *or* see recipe, p. 54
¼ cup salsa, *or* see recipe, p. 12
2 cups grated Monterey Jack or
    longhorn Cheddar cheese
    corn tortilla chips

Combine beans and salsa and heat until bubbly. Spread mixture over tortilla chips. Sprinkle cheese over bean mixture and place under broiler until cheese melts. Delicious served hot.

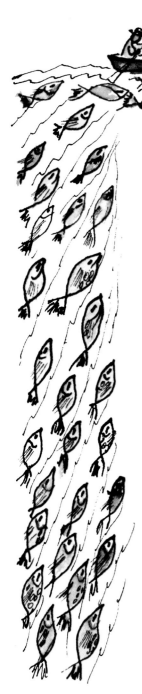

GUADALAJARA STUFFED SHRIMP ❧

Stuffed shrimp is delicious with a sprinkle of paprika and served with lemon slices.

1–2 pounds large shrimp
½ pound bacon, sliced
½ pound sharp Cheddar cheese
1 4-ounce can whole green chilies

Cook shrimp in boiling salted water until tender (3–5 minutes). Remove at once from boiling water and rinse with cold water. Shell and devein. Cut bacon slices in half so there is one-half slice for each shrimp. Fry bacon slightly. Cut cheese and chilies into narrow strips. Cut shrimp down back, but be careful not to cut all the way through. Stuff opened shrimp with a slice of cheese and a very thin slice of chili. Wrap with bacon and secure with wooden picks. Place on middle shelf in oven under broiler and cook until cheese melts and bacon is crisp. Serve at once.

YIELD: 6 servings

CHILI CON QUESO SQUARES

Mushrooms and olives may be substituted for chilies and onion for variety.

- 2 pounds longhorn Cheddar cheese, shredded
- 2 4-ounce cans chopped green chilies
- ¼ cup finely chopped onion
- 12 eggs, well beaten
- paprika

Spread half of cheese in the bottom of a greased 13 x 9 x 2-inch baking dish or pan. Sprinkle the chopped green chilies and chopped onion evenly over the cheese; cover with remaining cheese. Make sure eggs are beaten well; pour over cheese, chili, onion layers, and sprinkle with paprika. Bake in a 350 degree oven for 35–40 minutes or until a knife inserted in center comes out clean. Cut into squares. Delicious served warm.

Note: This appetizer may be served with toothpicks or eaten with fingers.

YIELD: Number of squares determined by desired size

GORDITAS

These little fat tortillas may be stuffed with other fillings to create a variety of appetizers.

    4 cups masa harina
    ¼ cup flour
    ½ teaspoon baking powder
    2 teaspoons salt
    ⅔ cup lard or vegetable shortening
    2⅔ cup warm water or broth
       cooking oil for deep fat frying

Mix masa harina with flour, baking powder, and salt. Whip lard until fluffy and cut into dry ingredients with pastry blender or fingers. Add water or broth and mix until the dough holds together well. Flour the palms of the hands lightly and roll the dough into 12–15 balls using approximately 2 tablespoons dough. Press the balls into flat round cakes 4 inches in diameter. Bake on a medium-hot, ungreased griddle or frying pan over medium-high heat for just a few minutes or until they begin to turn slightly brown. Remove cakes from griddle or frying pan and allow to cool until you can touch them. With your fingers, pinch a slight ridge around edge of each cake to form a little tart shell. This can be done ahead of time until ready to fry. Fry in hot cooking oil at 365 degrees for a few minutes or until lightly golden brown. Drain on paper towels.

FILLING:
- ½ pound ground beef or chorizo (removed from casings)
- 1 tablespoon cooking oil
- salt and pepper to taste
- 3 tablespoons chopped onion
- ⅛ teaspoon garlic powder
- 2 tablespoons chopped chilies, optional
- 1½ cups shredded lettuce
- 1 cup shredded Monterey Jack or Swiss cheese

Brown the beef or chorizo in oil. Add salt and pepper to taste. If using beef, add onion, garlic, and chilies, and cook until onion is tender. Drain off excess fat. Fill the base of Gordita with 1½ tablespoons meat. Sprinkle each with 1 tablespoon lettuce and 1 tablespoon cheese. If desired, top with a small amount of sauce.

GORDITA SAUCE:
- 1 8-ounce can tomato sauce
- 1 small onion, minced
- 1 clove garlic, minced
- ½ teaspoon oregano
- salt and pepper to taste
- 1 tablespoon wine vinegar
- 1½ teaspoons chili powder
- 2 tablespoons olive or cooking oil
- dash of Tabasco sauce

Combine all ingredients in a saucepan and simmer over medium heat for 20–30 minutes until slightly thickened. Allow to cool.

YIELD: 16–18 Gorditas

CHILI CON QUESO ✌

Delicious served over green beans, baked potatoes, and steaks.

- 2 green peppers, diced
- 1 onion, chopped
- 2 tablespoons shortening or oil
- 1 cup canned tomatoes, chopped and undrained
- 1 4-ounce can diced green chilies
- 1 teaspoon salt
- 1 teaspoon chili powder
- 2 cups grated Old English brand or Velveeta brand cheese

Sauté peppers and onion in shortening. Stir continuously while adding tomatoes, cook five minutes. Add green chilies, salt, chili powder, and cheese. Cook on low heat until cheese is melted. Serve hot with tortillas or corn chips. May be made ahead of time and reheated for serving.

SPICY PECANS

A nice holiday gift goodie!

- 4 tablespoons butter or margarine
- 4 tablespoons Worcestershire sauce
- 1 teaspoon salt
- ½ teaspoon ground cinnamon
- ⅛ teaspoon ground cloves
- ¼ teaspoon garlic powder
- ¼ teaspoon cayenne
- 1 pound pecan halves
  dash Tabasco sauce, optional

Melt butter or margarine in heavy skillet. Stir in rest of ingredients, except pecans. Mix well, add pecans; stir until nuts are well coated. Place in a single layer in an ungreased 15½ x 10½ x 1-inch baking pan. Toast pecans in a 300 degree oven 25–30 minutes or until nuts are brown and crisp. Stir frequently.

YIELD: 4 cups

DIPS AND SAUCES

SALSA

Versatile salsa may be used as a dip for corn chips and is adaptable to many types of dishes as a topping.

2 cups canned tomatoes,
    undrained and chopped
1 medium onion, chopped
2 cloves of garlic, minced
1 4-ounce can diced green chilies
½ teaspoon salt
1 tablespoon wine vinegar
1 green pepper, diced
½ teaspoon chili powder

Mix all ingredients together and cover. Leave overnight in refrigerator to blend flavors. If finer texture is desired, put ingredients in a blender for a few seconds.

GUACAMOLE

A delicious avocado mixture that may be served as a dip for crisp tortilla chips, a salad, a tortilla filling, or as a garnish.

2 large avocados
1 large tomato, chopped
¼ cup chopped onion
1 teaspoon lemon or other citrus juice
½ teaspoon salt
⅛ teaspoon pepper
⅛ teaspoon garlic powder
½ teaspoon Worcestershire sauce
⅛ teaspoon Tabasco sauce
½ cup sour cream
1 tablespoon mayonnaise (optional)

Peel and remove pit from avocado. Mash with fork. In bowl combine avocado, tomato, onion, lemon juice, salt, pepper, Tabasco sauce, garlic powder, Worcestershire sauce, sour cream, and mayonnaise. The lemon juice not only adds flavor but is a must to keep the avocado from discoloring. Delicious if made just before serving. Cover and chill. Serve as a dip for corn chips.

COLD BEAN DIP

Begin a hot spicy meal with the subtly seasoned flavor of this bean dip.

    1 15-ounce can refried beans
    1 teaspoon chili powder
    1 medium tomato, chopped
    2 tablespoons canned chopped green chilies
    ¼ teaspoon garlic powder
    1 cup sour cream
    ¼ cup sliced green onion, including some tops
    ½ cup shredded American cheese

Blend together refried beans with chili powder, tomatoes, green chili, and garlic powder. Mix well and combine with sour cream until thoroughly blended. Spoon into serving dish; garnish with sliced green onion and shredded cheese. Serve with tortilla chips.

    Note: 2 cups of your favorite refried beans may be used instead of canned beans.

YIELD: 3 cups

HOT BEAN DIP

Ingredients may be mixed in a blender, heated, then served in a chafing dish surrounded by corn chip "dippers."

- 2 cups refried beans
- 1 cup canned tomatoes, drained and chopped
- 1 tablespoon instant minced onion
- 1 teaspoon Worcestershire sauce
- 1 clove garlic, minced
- 1 teaspoon chili powder
- ¾ cup grated American or
      longhorn Cheddar cheese
   corn chips

Mix together all ingredients except corn chips. Heat until cheese melts, stirring occasionally. Serve warm, sprinkled with grated cheese, as a dip for corn chips.

CREAM CHEESE AND SALSA DIP

Colorful, zippy dip that is best made ahead of time to mellow flavors.

   1 7-ounce can green chili salsa, *or*
      see recipe, p. 12
   ½ teaspoon seasoned salt
   ¼ teaspoon garlic powder
   2 8-ounce packages cream cheese, softened
      chopped green onion for garnish
      corn chips

Combine salsa, salt, and garlic powder. Gradually add salsa mixture to softened cream cheese. Chill. Spoon into serving bowl and garnish with chopped green onions. Serve with corn chips.

Note: Just before serving, sprinkle with crushed salted peanuts for a crunchier taste.

YIELD: 2–3 cups

SOUPS

SOPA DE LIMA ⌑

Serve this flavorful soup piping hot with a sprinkle of grated cheese.

    3 chicken breasts
    6 cups chicken stock
    ¼ cup lime juice
    ½ cup lemon juice
    ¼ cup orange juice
    1 large white onion, quartered
    1 medium green bell pepper,
        cut in 1-inch pieces
    ¼ teaspoon cloves
    1 teaspoon salt
    1 teaspoon oregano
    ½ teaspoon black pepper
    ½ teaspoon parsley
    3 drops Tabasco sauce, optional
    1 1-pound can tomatoes, undrained
        and cut up
    5 tortillas
      cooking oil
    2 limes, thinly sliced

Combine chicken breasts, chicken stock, juices, onion, green pepper, and seasonings in a large saucepan and simmer until chicken is tender. While chicken is cooking, cut tortillas into 1-inch strips and fry in hot oil until they are crisp. Drain

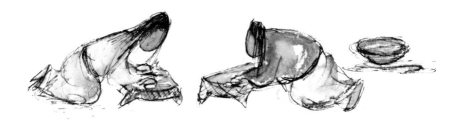

on paper towels. Set aside. When chicken is tender, remove meat from bones and cut into strips or bite-size pieces. Return meat to stock, add tomatoes and sliced limes. Simmer 10 minutes. To serve, divide tortillas equally in soup bowls. Add soup, making sure that one or two lime slices are in each bowl as a garnish.

YIELD: 6 servings

ALBONDIGAS SOUP

Some cooks like to alter the meatballs by placing some kind of "surprise" inside, such as an olive or chopped pine nuts.

BROTH:
- 1 small onion, minced
- 1 clove garlic, minced
- ¼ cup oil
- 1 8-ounce can tomato sauce
- 3 quarts beef stock or beef broth

ALBONDIGAS:
- ¾ pound ground beef
- ¾ pound ground pork
- ⅓ cup raw rice
- 1½ teaspoons salt
- ¼ teaspoon pepper
- 1 egg, slightly beaten

Sauté onion and garlic in oil. Add tomato sauce and beef stock and heat to boiling point. Meanwhile, mix ground meat with rice, egg, salt, and pepper, and shape into little balls. Drop into boiling broth. Cover and cook for 30 minutes.

GAZPACHO

Traditionally served chilled, gazpacho takes on a totally different and interesting flavor when heated.

- 8 cups tomato juice
- 6 tablespoons salad oil
- 4 tablespoons wine vinegar
- 1 teaspoon salt
- 1 teaspoon sugar
- 1 medium cucumber, chopped fine
- 1 medium to large onion, chopped fine
- 1 green pepper, chopped fine
- 2 cloves garlic, minced
- 2 tablespoons finely chopped parsley
- ¼ teaspoon pepper
- ½ teaspoon Worcestershire sauce
- 1 large tomato, chopped fine

Combine all ingredients in large bowl. Mix well. Cover and refrigerate overnight before serving. Garnish with croutons, chopped pimientos, diced avocado, or any choice of onions, green pepper, or cucumber. Gazpacho is better if made at least one day in advance; keeps well for several days in refrigerator.

midnight sketches
34 m DeGrazia 1982

MAIN DISHES

TACOS

This Mexican sandwich is delicious with cooked chorizo sausage, guacamole, chicken, refried beans, or your favorite filling.

- 1 pound ground beef or shredded roast beef
- 1 medium onion, chopped
- 1 clove garlic, minced
- 1 8-ounce can tomato sauce, optional
- ½ to 1 teaspoon salt
- ¼ teaspoon pepper
- 12 to 15 corn tortillas, see recipe, page 64
  shortening
- 2 cups grated longhorn Cheddar cheese
  shredded lettuce
- 1 large fresh tomato, chopped
  chopped scallions or green onions

Fry beef, add onion and garlic, sauté. Drain off excess fat, add tomato sauce if desired. Add salt and pepper. Meanwhile, in another skillet, fry tortillas in at least 2 inches of hot shortening. Using tongs or egg turner and fork, fold tortilla in half; immediately open to 45 degree angle. Continue frying until crisp. Drain on paper towels. Place 1 tablespoon of meat mixture in bottom of cooked tortilla. Top with lettuce, cheese, chopped tomato, and chopped scallions or green onions.

CHILI CON FRIJOLES

Serve this spiced stew garnished with grated Cheddar cheese and chopped scallions or green onions, or serve over fresh avocado shells.

- 2 pounds ground beef
- 1 medium onion, chopped
  cooking oil
- 1 teaspoon salt
- ½ teaspoon pepper
- 1 tablespoon chili powder
- ½ teaspoon cumin seed, optional
- 1 16-ounce can tomato sauce
- 1 28-ounce can tomatoes, undrained
- 2 15-ounce cans kidney or pinto beans, undrained

Cook ground beef and onion in small amount of hot oil until meat is brown. Drain off excess oil. Add seasonings, tomato sauce, and tomatoes that have been cut into pieces. Simmer for about 3 hours, stirring occasionally. Add beans and cook for about 45 minutes longer.

YIELD: 8 servings

TOSTADAS

A crisp-fried tortilla makes the bottom layer of what is really an open-faced sandwich—delicious, nutritious, and fun to eat.

- **6 corn tortillas**
- **½ cup shortening, lard, or cooking oil**
- **2 cups cooked mashed beans, hot**
- **½ cup grated American or**
  longhorn Cheddar cheese
  shredded lettuce
  chopped fresh tomatoes
  chopped scallions or green onions

Using tongs, immerse tortillas one at a time into hot shortening. Turn once while cooking until light brown. Drain on paper towels. Cover browned tortilla with hot mashed beans. Sprinkle with grated cheese, shredded lettuce, tomatoes, and scallions. Serve at once while still hot and crisp. Avocado slices are delicious as a garnish.

VARIATION:
This popular "sandwich" becomes a Beef Tostada with the addition of this delicious sauce.

- ¾ **pound ground beef**
- 1 **tablespoon olive oil**
- 1 **8-ounce can tomato sauce**
- ¼ **cup chopped onion**
- ¾ **teaspoon salt**
- 2 **teaspoons chili powder**
- ½ **teaspoon crushed oregano**
- ¼ **teaspoon garlic powder**
- ⅛ **teaspoon black pepper**

Brown beef in oil. Drain off excess fat and add tomato sauce, onion, salt, chili powder, oregano, garlic powder, and black pepper. Simmer 5 minutes, stirring frequently.

CHALUPAS

Cold, diced chicken or shrimp are delicious substitutes for the meat mixture. Try a dollop of guacamole for topping.

- 1 pound ground round
- ½ cup chopped onion
- 2 teaspoons chili powder
- ¼ cup chopped green bell pepper
- 1 tablespoon jalapeño pepper, optional
- 2 tablespoons flour
- ½ teaspoon salt
- ¼ teaspoon black pepper
- ½ cup water
- 2 cups refried pinto beans, fresh or canned
- 8 medium or 10 small corn tortillas
    cooking oil
- 2 cups grated longhorn Cheddar cheese
- 2 cups shredded lettuce
- 2 medium tomatoes, cut in small wedges
    or diced

Brown meat in a large skillet, drain off excess fat. Add onion, chili powder, green pepper, jalapeño pepper, flour, salt, and pepper. Stir occasionally and cook 8–10 minutes. Add water, cover and let simmer for 10 more minutes. Refry pinto beans in small amount of cooking oil to heat throughout. Place corn tortillas, flat, in hot oil and fry until crisp and firm. Drain on paper towels and place on an ungreased cookie sheet. Spread top of tortillas with refried beans. Top with meat mixture and sprinkle with grated cheese. Heat in 400 degree oven until cheese melts slightly. Remove from oven and sprinkle with shredded lettuce. Top with tomato and serve immediately while hot.

YIELD: 6–8 servings

ARROZ CON JACQUE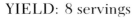

Sprinkle with sliced pimiento-stuffed olives just before serving.

- ¾ **pound Monterey Jack cheese**
- 3 **cups sour cream**
- 2 **4-ounce cans chopped green chilies**
- 3½ **cups cooked long grain rice**
  - **salt and pepper to taste**
- ⅔ **cup grated longhorn Cheddar cheese**

Cut Jack cheese into strips. Combine sour cream and chilies. Mix well. Grease a 1½-quart casserole. Season rice to taste with salt and pepper. In greased casserole dish, layer rice, chili mixture, and cheese strips. Repeat in that order, ending with rice on top. Bake at 350 degrees, 20–25 minutes. During last minutes of baking, remove from oven and sprinkle with grated Cheddar cheese. Return to oven to melt cheese.

YIELD: 8 servings

CHICKEN-CHILI BURRITOS

A crispy burrito recipe just waiting for your creativity in a topping.

    4 whole broiler-fryer chicken breasts
    2 tablespoons cooking oil
    1 large onion, chopped
    2 cloves garlic, chopped
    1 8-ounce can tomato sauce
    1 4-ounce can chopped green chilies
    2 tablespoons chili powder
    1 teaspoon salt
 1½ cups grated Monterey Jack cheese
    8 flour tortillas
      cooking oil for frying

Wash chicken, remove bone and skin, and cut into ½-inch pieces. Heat oil in large frying pan over medium heat. Add chicken, onion, and garlic. Sauté until onion is tender. Add tomato sauce, green chilies, chili powder, and salt. Cook about 35 minutes, stirring occasionally, until chicken is done and sauce is thickened. Spoon chicken mixture evenly onto tortillas. Top with a sprinkle of cheese. Roll tortillas into burritos by tucking up ends and overlapping sides. Secure with wooden picks. Heat cooking oil in a 3-quart saucepan or deep-fat fryer to approximately 375 degrees. Carefully add burritos in a single layer. Fry about 3 minutes, or until golden brown, turning when necessary. Drain on paper towels. Delicious served hot or cold.

YIELD: 8 servings.

GREEN CHILI BURROS

Delicious as a main dish. May also be made enchilada-style by covering with enchilada sauce, sprinkling with cheese, and heating.

    1 onion, chopped
    2 cups cooked ground beef or
        diced roast beef
    1 cup water or beef broth
    3 tablespoons flour
    1 4-ounce can diced green chilies
    2 tablespoons shortening
        salt and pepper to taste
        dash of garlic powder
    4 large flour tortillas, see recipe, page 62

Sauté onion in hot shortening. Add meat and seasonings. Mix together flour and water or broth. Add slowly to meat mixture, stirring often. When thickened, add chilies and mix well. Fill tortillas with meat mixture, roll toward you, fold sides in toward middle, and place seam down on heated plate. Serve warm.

   Burros become burritos by adding 1 cup refried beans to filling and frying folded tortilla in hot cooking oil until golden.

AVOCADO SALSA OMELET

A truly sumptuous dish that will win rave reviews at your next party brunch.

 6 eggs
 6 tablespoons cream or milk
 ½ teaspoon salt
  dash pepper
 2 tablespoons butter
 ½ cup grated longhorn Cheddar cheese
 1 ripe avocado, peeled, seeded, and diced
 4 slices bacon, chopped
 1 small onion, diced
 2 large tomatoes, peeled and diced
 ¼ teaspoon salt
 ⅛ teaspoon black pepper
 2 tablespoons canned diced green chilies
 ¼ teaspoon chili powder
 1 avocado, peeled and sliced for garnish

Beat eggs until fluffy. Add cream or milk and seasoning. Mix well. Melt butter over medium heat in omelet pan until it sizzles and becomes foamy. Pour omelet mixture into pan, while slowly turning pan over medium heat. With a fork, stir center of egg mixture, while cooking, in a figure 8 shape. Be sure to skim over top surface while stirring. As the underpart becomes set, slowly tilt pan and slightly lift omelet to allow uncooked part to flow underneath. Continue cooking until done and golden. Just before folding, sprinkle with cheese and add the avocado chunks across center of omelet. Fold omelet and remove to warm platter. Top with salsa and serve immediately.

Note: Eggs should be at room temperature before beating.

YIELD: 4 servings

FLAUTAS 🐦

A crunchy, tasty finger food. Another great way to use leftover roast beef or chicken!

1½ **cups cooked and shredded roast beef**
    or chicken
 1 **4-ounce can green chilies**
¼ **cup chopped onion**
12 **corn tortillas**
    cooking oil

Combine beef or chicken, chilies, and onion. Soften tortillas in hot cooking oil for a few seconds until pliable. Fill the tortillas with equal portions of mixture and roll tightly. Secure with wooden picks. Fry in hot oil until crisp. Serve plain or topped with guacamole.

Note: Flautas may be frozen after rolling, then thawed and fried crisp when ready to serve.

YIELD: 12 Flautas

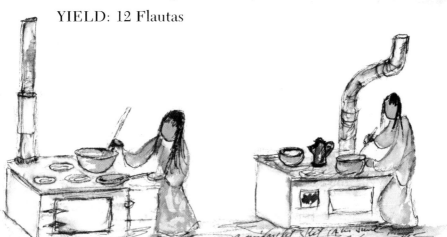

TAMALE PIE

All the flavor of tamales, but much less work.

CRUST:
- 4½ cups water
- 2 teaspoons salt
- 1 teaspoon chili powder
- 2¼ cups yellow corn meal

FILLING:
- 1 tablespoon shortening
- 1 pound lean ground beef
- 1 tablespoon chili powder
- 1 medium onion, chopped
- 1 clove garlic, minced
- 1 medium green bell pepper, chopped
- ½ cup chopped celery
- 1 cup sliced ripe olives
- 1 1-pound can tomatoes, undrained and cut up
- 1 16½-ounce can cream style corn
- 2 teaspoons salt
- 1 cup grated longhorn Cheddar cheese

CRUST DIRECTIONS:

Mix water, salt, chili powder, and corn meal in a saucepan over medium heat. Cook until very thick, stirring frequently. With a large spoon, line the sides and bottom of a greased 2-quart rectangular casserole with ⅔ of the corn meal mixture.

FILLING DIRECTIONS:

Melt the shortening in a large skillet. Brown meat in shortening. Add chili powder, onion, garlic, green pepper, and celery. Cook, while stirring, until onion is tender. Add remaining ingredients, except cheese. Simmer about 20 minutes, stirring frequently. Place filling in corn-meal-lined casserole. Top with remaining corn-meal mixture. Sprinkle with grated cheese. Bake in a 350 degree oven for 45 minutes or until done.

YIELD: 8 1¼-cup servings

FIESTA PIE

This is the Mexican version of what most *Norte-americanos* call a ground meat casserole.

½ cup minced onion
1 clove garlic, minced
½ cup chopped green bell pepper
1 tablespoon melted butter or margarine
1 pound ground round
¼ pound pork sausage
1 16-ounce can tomatoes
1 16-ounce can whole kernel corn, drained
1½ teaspoons salt
1½ teaspoons chili powder
½ cup sliced ripe olives
1 cup corn meal
1 cup milk
2 eggs, well beaten
1½ cups grated longhorn Cheddar cheese

Preheat oven to 350 degrees. Sauté onion, garlic, and bell pepper in melted butter over medium heat until onion is tender. Add meats and brown, while stirring. Pour off excess fat. Add vegetables and seasonings. Simmer uncovered while stirring, 2–3 minutes. Pour meat mixture into a buttered 2-quart casserole dish. Sprinkle with olives. Combine corn meal, milk, eggs, and half of grated cheese. Spoon over meat mixture and olives. Sprinkle with rest of grated cheese. Bake 1 hour in 350 degree oven.

YIELD: 6 servings

COFFEE TACO CASSEROLE

A taco becomes a *cacerola* in this flavorful dish that's just waiting for dollops of sour cream and a sprinkle of ripe olives.

 1½ pounds lean ground beef
 1 medium onion, chopped
 2 teaspoons powdered instant coffee
 1 teaspoon chili powder
 1 teaspoon salt
 ¼ teaspoon pepper
 ¼ teaspoon oregano
 ⅛ teaspoon garlic powder
 2 8-ounce cans tomato sauce
 8 small corn tortillas
 1 3-ounce package cream cheese, softened
 1 cup grated longhorn Cheddar cheese

Brown beef and onion in skillet; pour off fat. Stir in coffee, chili powder, salt, pepper, oregano, garlic powder, and 1 can tomato sauce; simmer while stirring 5 minutes. Spread one side of each tortilla with softened cream cheese, then top with some of meat mixture. Fold in half; overlap in shallow baking dish, open side up. Fill in spaces around tortillas with remaining meat mixture. Pour on remaining can of tomato sauce. Sprinkle with grated cheese. Bake at 350 degrees for 20 minutes.

YIELD: 4 servings.

CHILI-CHICKEN CON CARNE

1 medium onion, chopped
1 clove garlic, minced
2 tablespoons cooking oil
2 tablespoons chopped green chilies
2 16-ounce cans tomatoes, undrained and broken up
1 8-ounce can tomato sauce
1½ teaspoons chili powder
½ teaspoon salt
⅛ teaspoon black pepper
½ teaspoon oregano
1 teaspoon Worcestershire sauce
1 1-pound, 4-ounce can kidney beans, undrained
2 cups cooked, diced chicken
4 cups cooked rice

In a large saucepan sauté onion and garlic in oil for 5 minutes or until tender. Add chilies, tomatoes, tomato sauce, chili powder, salt, pepper, oregano, and Worcestershire sauce. Simmer uncovered, 15–20 minutes, stirring occasionally. Add kidney beans and chicken. Heat at least 5 minutes. Serve over hot cooked rice.

Note: For a spicier flavor, add a few drops of Tabasco sauce. Turkey could be substituted for chicken.

YIELD: 6 servings

PICADILLO STUFFED ONIONS

Mexican-flavored stuffed onions make an attractive lunch with a favorite salad.

- 3 sweet Spanish onions
- 1 pound lean ground beef
- 1 clove garlic, minced
- 2 tablespoons butter or margarine
- 1 8-ounce can tomatoes, undrained and cut up
- 2 tablespoons wine vinegar
- ½ teaspoon sugar
- ½ teaspoon cinnamon
- ¼ teaspoon cumin
- 1 teaspoon salt
- dash of ground cloves
- 1 tablespoon chili powder
- ½ cup raisins, plumped in ¼ cup hot water
- ¼ cup slivered almonds

Peel and halve onions. Boil in salted water 10 minutes until tender. Drain. Remove centers, leaving ¾-inch shells. Chop centers and set aside. Brown ground beef, chopped onion, and garlic in butter or margarine. Drain off any excess fat. Add remaining ingredients except almonds. Simmer 25–30 minutes, stirring often. Spoon into onion shells. Bake, covered, in 350 degree oven for 20–25 minutes. Remove, uncover, sprinkle with almonds, and bake 5–10 minutes longer.

YIELD: 6 servings

CHILI QUESO QUICHE

Spicy fillings covered with delicately flavored custard make up this Mexican quiche.

- 1 10-inch pie shell, uncooked
- 1 7-ounce can whole green chilies
- 1 small onion, sliced
- 1 pound pork sausage, cooked and crumbled
- 4 eggs, lightly beaten
- 2 cups light cream or half-and-half
- 1 cup grated Swiss cheese
- ¼ cup grated Parmesan cheese
- ¼ teaspoon salt
- ⅛ teaspoon garlic powder
- ¼ teaspoon chili powder

Line bottom of pie shell with whole chilies that have been split open, seeded, and flattened. Top with onion slices and sprinkle with cooked sausage. Combine eggs, cream, cheeses, and seasonings; pour over sausage. Bake in a preheated 350 degree oven for 35–40 minutes or until top is golden brown and quiche is set. Remove from oven and allow to cool for 5 minutes before serving.

YIELD: 6 servings

CHILI SOUFFLÉ

A sprinkle of sliced olives and chopped green onions is delicious as a garnish for this easy-to-prepare soufflé.

  1 **pound sharp Cheddar cheese, grated**
  1 **7-ounce can diced green chilies**
  1 **pound mild Cheddar cheese, grated**
  1 **pound Monterey Jack cheese, grated**
 12 **eggs**
1½ **cups sour cream**

Put layer of sharp Cheddar cheese in bottom of buttered 2½-quart casserole and add a layer of chilies. Add a layer of mild Cheddar cheese, another of chilies. Top with a layer of Monterey Jack cheese. Beat eggs well and stir in sour cream. Pour over mixture in casserole and bake in a 325 degree oven 35–45 minutes or until golden brown.

Note: Allow guests to help themselves to a topping of salsa.

YIELD: 6 servings

CHIMICHANGAS ✎

A delicious version of the popular burro, served on a bed of shredded lettuce and topped with sour cream and guacamole.

- 6 large flour tortillas
- 1 pound lean ground beef
- 1 medium onion, chopped
- ½ cup salsa or enchilada sauce,
    see recipes, pp. 12, 29
    cooking oil
- 1 cup guacamole, see recipe, page 13
- 1 cup sour cream
    shredded lettuce and chopped scallions
    or green onions

Prepare filling by browning ground beef and adding onion. Cook until soft. Moisten with desired sauce. Simmer for 10 minutes, stirring occasionally.

Spoon filling down center of tortilla. Fold tortilla around filling, and fold sides in toward middle. Fasten with wooden picks.

Fry in hot oil over medium heat, turning, until golden; takes 1–2 minutes. Lift with tongs from cooking oil, drain on paper towels. To serve, place on shredded lettuce bed, top with dollops of guacamole and sour cream. Sprinkle with chopped scallions or green onions.

QUESADILLAS

The delicious milk flavor makes a perfect entrée for those who don't ordinarily like spicy Mexican food.

12 regular size flour tortillas
1 7-ounce can whole green chilies,
   seeds and pits removed
1 pound Monterey Jack cheese, sliced
1 pound Cheddar cheese, sliced
1 cup butter or margarine for frying

To make each Quesadilla, separate flour tortillas and place about ¼ of a green chili in the center of each tortilla. Next, arrange a thick slice (about 1 x 4 x ½-inch) of Jack and Cheddar cheese side by side on one half of tortilla. Fold tortilla over cheese and pin shut with a small wooden pick. Fry in shallow hot butter until golden brown, turning occasionally. Be careful not to burn butter or Quesadilla. Drain on paper towels and serve hot.

Note: Delicious served with favorite salsa as a topping.

YIELD: 12 Quesadillas

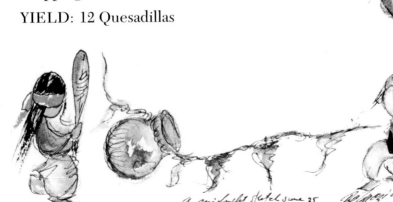

ENSALADA DE NOCHE BUENA ❧

A traditional salad served on Christmas Eve. Usually garnished with only a sprinkle of sugar or orange juice. Great for Navidad, the happiest and most colorful Mexican festival.

> 3 medium beets, cooked, peeled, and sliced
>   or 1 16-ounce can sliced beets, drained
> 3 oranges, peeled, white membrane
>   removed
> 3 red apples, unpeeled and cored
> 3 bananas, peeled
> 3 limes, peeled, white membrane removed
> 1 fresh pineapple, peeled and cored,
>   or 1 1-pound, 14-ounce can
>   pineapple chunks
> 2 carrots, cut in strips
> 1 head lettuce, shredded or torn into pieces
> 1 tablespoon sugar
> 1 cup chopped peanuts
>   seeds of 2 pomegranates
>   jicama, optional

Thinly slice the beets, oranges, apples, bananas, limes, and pineapple (if using fresh). Cut carrots into strips. Toss apples and bananas in orange juice to prevent fruit from discoloring. Line serving platter or large shallow bowl with lettuce. Drain apples and bananas and arrange along with rest of fruit, beets, jicama, and carrots on top of lettuce. Sprinkle with sugar, peanuts, and pomegranate seeds.

Note: If desired, drizzle salad with French dressing, orange juice, or with mayonnaise/salad dressing thinned with a little milk. Mix gently just before serving.

YIELD: 8 servings

TACO SALAD

- 1 **pound lean ground beef**
- 4 **tablespoons green chilies**
- 1 **16-ounce can tomatoes, undrained and** **cut up in pieces**
- 1 **head lettuce, shredded**
- 2 **medium tomatoes, diced**
- ½ **cup grated Cheddar or American cheese**
- 3 **whole green onions including tops, chopped**
- 2 **cups small corn chips**
- 1 **cup kidney beans, optional**
- 2 **tablespoons sliced ripe olives**

Brown hamburger, drain off excess fat. Season with salt, pepper, and garlic salt to taste; add green chilies and canned tomatoes; cook uncovered about 30 minutes to reduce liquid; stir occasionally. In a separate bowl combine lettuce, tomatoes, cheese, onions, kidney beans, and olives. Toss gently. Top with cooked ground beef and corn chips. Toss well. Serve immediately.

YIELD: 8 servings

TOPOPO

This mountain-shaped dish is a Mexican counter-part to a hearty chef's salad.

    2 10-inch corn tortillas
    ⅔ cup warm refried beans
    2 cups shredded lettuce
    ½ cup cold cooked ham, sliced in thin strips
    ½ cup diced longhorn or mild Cheddar cheese
    1 cup cold cooked turkey or chicken, sliced
    1 ripe avocado, peeled, pitted, and sliced
    1 4-ounce can diced green chilies
    ¼ cup shredded Romano cheese
    ½ cup sliced pimiento-stuffed olives
       tomato wedges

Heat 1-inch salad oil in a frying pan to 350 de-grees. Fry one tortilla at a time, using tongs to turn frequently, until it becomes crisp and lightly browned on each side. Drain on paper towels. Spread generously with warm refried beans. Pile lettuce on beans. Arrange alternate strips of ham, cheese, and turkey around the sides; fill in the center by forming a peak with avocado slices. Sprinkle with olives and chili peppers. Spoon Romano cheese on the tip of the peak and top with tomato wedge. Serve at once with Topopo Dressing.

YIELD: 2 Topopos

TOPOPO DRESSING:
- ⅔ **cup corn oil**
- ⅓ **cup wine vinegar**
- 1 **teaspoon salt**
- 1 **teaspoon dark corn syrup**
- ½ **teaspoon paprika**
- ½ **teaspoon dry mustard**
- ¼ **teaspoon black pepper**
- ⅛ **teaspoon Tabasco sauce**

Mix all ingredients in bowl; chill. Mix well before serving.

YIELD: 1 cup

CHICKEN TAMALES

Delicious served with a topping of taco sauce and sour cream.

    1 large broiler chicken
    1 large onion, sliced
    3 cloves garlic, whole
    2 tablespoons cooking oil
    1 cup finely chopped onion
    1 large green bell pepper,
        seeded and chopped
    1 4-ounce can chopped green chilies
        salt and pepper to taste

Combine chicken, garlic, and sliced onion in enough water to cover; cook until done. Remove chicken from broth and cut into small pieces; reserve broth. Sauté the chopped onion and pepper in cooking oil until the pepper is tender. Remove from heat and add chilies and chicken. Season with salt and pepper to taste.

MASA:
    1 cup lard or soft margarine or butter
    3 cups masa harina
    1 teaspoon salt
    ½ teaspoon baking powder
    1¾ cups strained chicken broth
        corn husks

With an electric mixer, whip shortening until fluffy and blend in other ingredients. Beat until dough holds together well and is light and airy. This can be tested by putting (not dropping) a small piece of the dough onto the surface of a cup of water. If it floats, it has been mixed long enough. If not, mix more and test later.

HUSKS:
Soak husks in warm water for about an hour; drain and pat dry with paper towels to remove excess moisture. Flatten out the husks; on the center of each one put 1½ tablespoons of dough. Spread out dough in the center of the husk, leaving room to fold over the ends at top and bottom. Tear another husk into thin strips to tie the ends shut. Put about 1½ tablespoons of filling on top of corn mixture and roll or fold the corn husks so that the corn mixture is covered. Fold down the ends slightly or tie with strips of corn husks or string. Repeat until masa and filling are used. (Filling should be completely covered by the dough.) Place the tamales in a steamer or on a rack in an electric skillet. Add water to just below rack level. Bring to boiling; cover and steam for 40–45 minutes or until tamale pulls away from corn husk when tested. Add water as needed.

YIELD: 20 medium tamales

HUEVOS RANCHEROS

A real eye opener!

     2 tablespoons butter or margarine
     ½ cup chopped green onion,
           including some tops
     ½ cup chopped green bell pepper
     1 clove garlic, minced
     ¼ cup canned diced green chilies
     1 28-ounce can tomatoes, undrained
           and cut up
     1 teaspoon salt
     ½ teaspoon sugar
     ⅛ teaspoon black pepper
     1 teaspoon crushed cilantro or dried parsley
     6 corn tortillas
           butter or margarine, melted
     6 eggs
     1 cup shredded longhorn Cheddar cheese
     1 large avocado, peeled, pitted, sliced thin

Melt butter; add onion, green pepper, and garlic
and sauté until tender. Add chilies, tomatoes,
salt, sugar, pepper, and cilantro or parsley. Simmer, uncovered, 15 minutes or until sauce is reduced and thickened slightly. Heat tortillas one
at a time in melted butter or margarine until
slightly golden on each side. Be careful not to fry
until crisp; tortillas should be soft. Keep warm on
oven proof platter, covered with foil. (Do not
hold longer than it takes to fry eggs or tortillas
will toughen.) Fry eggs in butter or margarine,

sunny-side up. Place an egg in center of each tortilla; surround with 1-inch-wide ring of tomato sauce mixture. Sprinkle with cheese. Garnish with slices of avocado. Serve at once. Pass extra sauce in separate bowl.

YIELD: 6 servings

CHICKEN ENCHILADAS

A wonderful way to use leftover chicken.

  1 **cup boned chicken**
½ **cup chicken broth or water**
  1 **4-ounce can diced green chilies**
½ **cup chopped onion**
  1 **10-ounce can cream of chicken soup**
  1 **cup grated longhorn Cheddar cheese**
¼ **teaspoon pepper**
  6 **corn tortillas**
    vegetable oil

Mix together soup, broth, chilies, and pepper. Set aside. Soften tortillas by dipping one at a time into hot oil. Drain tortillas on paper towels and stack.

Mix chicken and onion together. Put 2 tablespoons chicken mixture in center of each tortilla. Sprinkle with grated cheese and roll up. Place in shallow baking dish. Continue until all tortillas are rolled. Pour soup mixture over top and sprinkle with remaining grated cheese. Bake 10–15 minutes in 375 degree oven.

SOUR CREAM ENCHILADAS 🐚

Tortillas may be rolled, folded, or stacked when making these delicious enchiladas.

- 1 10-ounce can enchilada sauce
- 1 16-ounce can whole tomatoes, undrained and chopped
- ⅓ cup chopped onion
- ½ teaspoon salt
- 12 corn tortillas
  cooking oil
- 1½ cups grated longhorn Cheddar cheese
- 1½ cups sour cream

In saucepan combine enchilada sauce, tomatoes, onion, and salt. Heat over medium flame until mixture boils. Heat oil in small skillet until hot. Dip one tortilla at a time in hot oil for several seconds. Drain tortilla on paper towels. Continue until all tortillas have been softened. On each tortilla place a heaping tablespoon of sauce and sprinkle with grated cheese. Roll up and place in shallow casserole dish, seam side down, close together. Pour remaining sauce over enchiladas. Sprinkle with additional grated cheese. Heat in oven at 400 degrees for 15 minutes. Spoon sour cream over enchiladas and serve hot.

BEEF ENCHILADAS

Enchilada excellence depends largely on the filling and sauce used. Possible variations include meat, poultry, shredded cheese, onion, refried beans, chili, hard-cooked eggs, guacamole, and sour cream.

- 1 pound ground beef or shredded beef
- 1 medium onion, chopped
- 2 teaspoons chili powder
- 1 teaspoon salt
- 2 tablespoons fat
- 12 corn tortillas
- ½ pound grated American or longhorn Cheddar cheese
- 1 medium onion, chopped
- 2 cups enchilada sauce

ENCHILADA SAUCE:
- 2 cups tomato sauce
- 2 cups water
- 4 teaspoons dried minced onions
- 2 bouillon cubes
- ½ teaspoon salt
- ½ teaspoon garlic powder
- 1 teaspoon chili powder

Mix sauce ingredients, simmer for 5 minutes.

Cook beef in fat, add onion, chili powder, and salt. Soften tortillas by dipping one at a time in hot enchilada sauce. Spoon on filling, roll, then arrange in shallow baking dish, seam side down. Pour on remaining enchilada sauce, sprinkle with onion and cheese. Heat at 350 degrees for 15–20 minutes or until cheese melts.

GUISADO

1½ pounds ground round
½ cup dry bread crumbs
½ cup grated longhorn Cheddar cheese
   juice of 1 lemon
⅛ teaspoon garlic powder
1 egg, beaten slightly
1 tablespoon parsley
1 teaspoon salt
2 tablespoons butter, margarine,
   or cooking oil
1 cup all-purpose flour
1 cup hot water
1½ cups tomato sauce
1 teaspoon chili powder
¼ teaspoon oregano
¼ teaspoon black pepper
1 cup elbow macaroni, cooked

Combine meat, bread crumbs, cheese, lemon juice, garlic, egg, parsley, and salt. Form into balls the size of large walnuts. Melt butter in heavy frying pan or electric skillet. Brown meatballs quickly on all sides. Dredge browned meatballs in flour; brown again. Add water, tomato sauce, chili powder, oregano, and black pepper. Cover; simmer slowly for 1 hour. Remove cover and add cooked macaroni. Simmer together for 2–3 minutes to heat macaroni thoroughly. Serve on large hot platter garnished with grated longhorn Cheddar cheese.

Note: If macaroni is omitted, you'll find this

flavorful meat mixture is also delicious served over cooked rice.

YIELD: 6–8 servings

CHILIES RELLENOS

Chilies rellenos, "stuffed peppers," are usually stuffed with cheese to become chilies rellenos con queso. Other fillings may be used—including meat, seafood, and beans.

- 2 4-ounce cans green chilies
- 1 pound Monterey Jack or longhorn
     Cheddar cheese
- 4 eggs
- 4 tablespoons flour
- 1 cup cooking oil
     chopped scallions or green onions
     canned or homemade salsa

Split green chilies enough to allow insertion of cheese cut into half-inch strips. Dredge stuffed chilies in flour. Separate eggs. Beat egg whites until stiff peaks form. Beat egg yolks until creamy. Fold yolks into whites, adding flour as you fold. Dip each stuffed chili into batter and set on small dish. Add additional batter on top of chilies to cover well. Slide coated chilies from dish into hot oil and fry until golden brown, about 2 minutes. Turn once gently. Drain on paper towels. Season with salt and pepper to taste. Serve hot, immediately after cooking, with garnish of grated cheese and chopped scallion or green onion, or canned or homemade salsa Serve with rice and refried beans.

51

RITA LA RUBIA
COMIDA MEJICANA

EMPANADAS DE POLLO

Pastry turnovers with a savory chicken filling.

½ cup chopped onion
1 clove garlic, minced
2 tablespoons butter or margarine
1 8-ounce can tomato sauce
½ cup water
½ teaspoon chili powder
1½ cups chopped cooked chicken
¼ cup chopped raisins
½ cup chopped blanched almonds
¼ teaspoon salt
1 egg, slightly beaten
2 cups all-purpose flour
1 teaspoon salt
⅔ cup shortening
5–6 tablespoons cold water

Cook onion and garlic in butter or margarine until tender. Add tomato sauce, water, and chili powder; simmer for 15 minutes. Combine mixture with chicken, raisins, almonds, ¼ teaspoon salt, and egg; set aside. To make pastry, mix flour and 1 teaspoon salt; cut in shortening with pastry blender, two forks, or fingers, to size of peas. Sprinkle in water, while mixing with fork, until dough holds together when pressed. Roll out pastry on lightly floured board to ⅛-inch thickness. Cut into 8, 6-inch circles. Spoon ¼ cup filling over half of each circle. Fold the other half over; wet the edges with water and press firmly with a fork to seal in the filling. Bake at 400 degrees for 25–30 minutes or until golden brown. If desired, serve with Empanada Sauce while warm.

EMPANADA SAUCE:
  1 onion, chopped
  1 clove garlic, minced
  2 tablespoons butter or margarine
1¾ cups canned tomatoes, undrained
      and cut up
  1 8-ounce can tomato sauce
  1 teaspoon Worcestershire sauce
    salt and pepper to taste

Sauté onion and garlic in butter or margarine until tender. Add other ingredients and simmer 45 minutes or until reduced and thickened.

YIELD: 8 servings

MIDNIGHT SKECH
JUNE 1AM 1976

VEGETABLES

FRIJOLES REFRITOS

Next to corn, the frijole (bean) is the most common ingredient in Mexican cooking.

  1 pound pinto beans (frijoles)
  ¼ pound salt pork
  1 teaspoon chili powder
  1 clove garlic, finely chopped
  ½ teaspoon salt
  2 tablespoons shortening
  1 cup grated longhorn Cheddar cheese

Soak frijoles in water overnight. Next day pour off water; cover frijoles with boiling water. Add salt pork; cook slowly until tender, about 4 hours. Add additional water as needed. Add chili powder, garlic, and salt. Simmer 30 minutes. Remove all but 1 cup of liquid.

Mash beans until smooth. Melt shortening in large skillet; add frijoles and fry over medium heat, stirring occasionally. To serve, place frijoles in a large bowl and top with grated cheese.

YIELD: 6 to 8 servings

MEXICAN VEGETABLE RICE

This rice dish is delicious served with your favorite chicken or shrimp recipe.

    2 cups long grain rice
    2 large tomatoes, peeled and chopped
    ½ cup chopped onion
    1 clove garlic, minced
    ⅛ teaspoon chili powder
    ⅛ teaspoon oregano
    4 tablespoons cooking oil
 3½ cups boiling chicken stock or broth
    1 green bell pepper, chopped
    ¾ cup thinly sliced carrots
    1 cup green peas, fresh or thawed frozen
    1 tablespoon chopped fresh coriander or
        parsley

Rinse rice, if desired, and allow to dry. Place tomatoes, onion, garlic, chili powder, and oregano in a blender and purée at high speed. Heat oil in a medium skillet, add rice and sauté, stirring constantly, until golden in color. Add the tomato mixture and cook, stirring occasionally, until all moisture has evaporated. Pour this mixture into a covered 3-quart casserole and add chicken stock, bell pepper, carrots, and peas. Mix well and cook in a 350 degree oven for 35 minutes or until the rice is dry and all the liquid is absorbed. Garnish with chopped coriander or parsley and serve while warm.

YIELD: 8 servings

FRIJOLES CON QUESO

Leftover beans won't be leftover again when prepared in this spicy manner.

3 slices bacon
1 cup chopped green bell pepper
½ cup chopped onion
1 clove garlic, minced
1 teaspoon crushed oregano leaves
1 teaspoon salt
1 tablespoon chili powder
1 tablespoon cilantro or parsley
1 cup canned tomatoes, undrained and cut up
½ cup tomato sauce
2 cups red kidney beans or pinto beans, cooked or canned
1 cup shredded longhorn cheese

Fry bacon until crisp; drain, crumble, and set aside. Sauté green pepper, onion, and garlic in bacon fat until tender. Add seasonings, tomatoes, tomato sauce, and 1 cup of the beans. Mash the remaining 1 cup beans and add to mixture. Cook slowly for 15–20 minutes, while stirring, until sauce has thickened. Blend in cheese. Stir until melted. Top with crumbled bacon and serve while hot.

Note: Serve as a side dish or as a dip with corn chips

YIELD: 6 servings

PAPAS CON QUESO ✎

Lazy cooks enjoy putting this one together!

  4 cups sliced potatoes
  2 cloves garlic, minced
  ⅓ cup chopped green chilies
  2 cups tomato sauce
  1 teaspoon chili powder
1½ teaspoons salt
  ¼ teaspoon oregano
  1 tablespoon chili sauce, optional
  1 cup grated longhorn Cheddar cheese

Place potatoes in 2½-quart buttered casserole dish. Mix remaining ingredients, except cheese, and pour over potatoes. Bake, covered, in a 350 degree oven until potatoes are tender; about 1 hour. Remove from oven, sprinkle with cheese, return to oven uncovered, and cook until cheese is melted and slightly browned on top.

Note: A sprinkle of chopped green onion just before serving adds great flavor and color.

YIELD: 6 servings

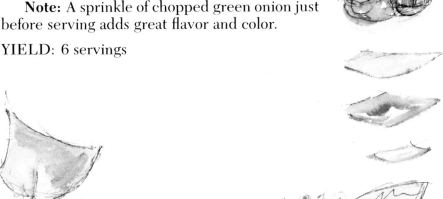

MEXICAN CORN PUDDING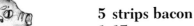

A festive spoon bread to brighten your next dinner party. Serve as a vegetable or as a substitute for bread.

　　5　strips bacon
　　1　17-ounce can cream-style corn
　　2　eggs, well beaten
　　2　cups milk
　　1　cup yellow corn meal
　　1　teaspoon baking powder
　　1　teaspoon salt
1½　cups grated longhorn Cheddar cheese
　¼　cup chopped green chilies
　　2　tablespoons minced onion
　　　pinch of garlic powder

Fry bacon until crisp. Crumble and set aside. Reserve 5 tablespoons bacon drippings. Except for bacon and ½ cup grated cheese, combine remaining ingredients in a large mixing bowl and mix well. Pour into a well greased 3-quart casserole. Sprinkle reserved bacon and cheese on top. Bake in a 350 degree oven 1 hour or until a knife inserted in center comes out clean.

Note: If cheese topping begins to brown too much, cover loosely with a sheet of aluminum foil.

YIELD: 8 servings

MEXICAN SKILLET CORN

A flavorful combination of textures and color that goes well with many main dishes.

3 slices bacon
3 cups drained corn, fresh cut or
    canned whole kernel
½ cup chopped green bell pepper
¼ cup finely chopped onion
¼ cup chopped pimiento
¼ teaspoon chili powder
½ teaspoon salt
⅛ teaspoon pepper

Fry bacon until crisp. Remove from drippings, drain, crumble, and set aside. Add vegetables and chili powder to drippings; stir, cover, and cook over low heat for 15–20 minutes or until corn is tender. (Stir occasionally to keep from sticking.) Add salt and pepper, mix well. Pour into serving dish, sprinkle with crumbled bacon. Serve hot.

YIELD: 6 servings

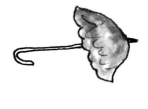

MEXICAN CORN CASSEROLE

Serve piping hot straight from the oven.

⅓ cup melted butter or margarine
2 eggs, slightly beaten
1 cup cream-style corn
1 cup cottage cheese
1 cup corn meal
2 teaspoons baking powder
1 teaspoon salt
1 4-ounce can chopped green chilies
¼ cup sliced stuffed green olives
1 cup grated longhorn Cheddar cheese

In a large mixing bowl combine butter, eggs, corn, and cottage cheese. In a separate bowl combine corn meal, baking powder, and salt. Add to corn mixture. Pour one-half of batter into a greased 8 x 10-inch baking dish. Layer the green chilies on the batter along with sliced olives and half of the grated cheese. Pour the remainder of the batter in dish and top with rest of the cheese. Bake in a 350 degree oven for 1 hour.

YIELD: 6 servings

SPANISH RICE

This tomato-flavored rice is found served as a side dish along with refried beans in most Mexican homes.

1 medium green pepper, chopped
1 small onion, chopped
3 tablespoons cooking oil
1 cup long grain rice
2 cups canned tomatoes
2 cups water
salt and pepper to taste

Sauté green pepper and onion in oil. Add rice and cook until rice is golden brown, stirring frequently. Add tomatoes and water; salt and pepper to taste. Cover, reduce heat, and simmer until all water is used and rice is flaky.

Note: Toast rice in hot oil to enhance flavor and to separate and fluff.

YIELD: 6 to 8 servings

BREADS

FLOUR TORTILLAS

This "little cake" has been a Mexican staple since the Spaniards introduced wheat flour hundreds of years ago.

  4 cups flour
1½ teaspoons salt
  ½ cup lard or vegetable shortening
  1 cup warm water

Cut in lard or shortening with pastry blender or with fingers until coarse. Dissolve salt in water and gradually add to flour mixture. Knead dough well, cover, and set aside (not in refrigerator) for 2–3 hours to improve elasticity of dough.

Knead dough again and divide into 10 balls. Roll each ball out on floured board to ⅛-inch thickness. Place tortilla on moderately hot *ungreased* griddle for about 20 seconds. Flip over and cook for a few seconds on other side. Cook until slightly brown in spots.

YIELD: 10 flour tortillas

SOPAIPILLAS

A deep-fried bread that puffs up like little pillows to produce a delicious change from tortillas.

    4 cups flour
1½ teaspoons salt
    4 teaspoons baking powder
    4 tablespoons shortening
1½ to 2 cups water

Sift together dry ingredients. Add shortening and cut in coarsely with pastry blender or fork. Add enough water to make soft, but not sticky, dough. Knead gently on floured board. Roll into rectangle ¼-inch thick. Let sit to rise for 5–10 minutes. Cut into 3-inch squares. Fry in deep fat until puffy and golden. Drain on paper towels. If used as dessert, sprinkle with powdered sugar or drizzle with honey.

CORN TORTILLAS

The most versatile bread of all—may be stacked, rolled, folded, torn, cut, or crumbled.

> **2 cups masa harina**
> **1 teaspoon salt**
> **1¼ cups cold water (approximately)**

Combine flour, salt, and water; knead to blend well; set aside for 15 minutes—do not refrigerate. Shape dough into walnut-sized pieces. Roll very thin or press each ball between 2 sheets of waxed paper to form a 6-inch circle. Bake on hot, *ungreased* griddle. In a few seconds the edges will begin to dry out; at this point turn tortilla and let cook for slightly longer period until second side is slightly browned. Then flip back onto the first side and let it finish cooking; whole process should take about 2 minutes.

YIELD: 12 to 14 corn tortillas

MEXICAN CORN BREAD ❧

Pastel de elote, "corn pie," is what most *Norte-americanos* call corn bread.

 1 cup corn meal
 ½ teaspoon soda
 ¾ teaspoon salt
 1 small–medium onion, chopped
 1 cup cream-style corn
 ¼ cup bacon drippings or cooking oil
 2 eggs
 1 clove garlic, chopped
 1 cup sour cream or milk
 1 small jalapeño pepper, minced
 1 cup grated Cheddar cheese

Mix corn meal, soda, salt, onion, garlic, corn, oil, sour cream, and eggs. Beat well. Spread half of mixture in greased 10-inch iron skillet or baking pan. Spread pepper and cheese over batter. Cover with remaining batter. Bake 45 minutes at 350 degrees. May be made ahead of time and reheated before serving.

YIELD: 10 servings

DESSERTS

CHOCOLATE ALMENDRADO ❧

A light, airy dessert flavored with almonds and rum, topped with a rich sauce.

   1 tablespoon plain gelatin
¼ cup cold water
   1 cup boiling water
   1 cup sugar
   4 egg whites (reserve yolks for sauce)
   1 tablespoon rum or 1 teaspoon
      rum flavoring
   2 tablespoons cocoa
¾ cup ground almonds

Soften gelatin in cold water; pour boiling water over gelatin; add sugar and stir until dissolved. Let cool, then chill until slightly firm. Beat egg whites until stiff; fold into gelatin. Add rum. Divide in half and mix cocoa into one portion. Spoon into a lightly oiled 4-cup mold, alternating white and chocolate layers and sprinkling ground almonds between layers. Chill until firm (several hours or overnight). To serve, unmold dessert onto serving plate and spoon chilled Custard Sauce over top. Cut into wedges.

CUSTARD SAUCE:
   4 egg yolks
¼ cup sugar
⅛ teaspoon salt
   2 cups milk
   2 tablespoons rum or 1½ teaspoons
      rum flavoring

Beat egg yolks and sugar together. Add salt and milk. Cook in top of double boiler over simmering water, stirring frequently. When custard has thickened, stir in 2 tablespoons rum or 1½ teaspoons rum flavoring.

YIELD: 6 servings

EMPANADAS DE FRUTA ❧

A delicious, spicy, south-of-the-border "turnover" that is a proper finish for any meal.

CRUST:

  1½ **cups flour**
    1 **teaspoon baking powder**
    1 **teaspoon salt**
    8 **tablespoons shortening**
  4–6 **tablespoons water**

Sift flour with baking powder and salt. Cut in shortening and mix well. Add enough water to make easy-to-handle dough. Roll out dough ⅛-inch thick. Cut in circles about 3 inches in diameter.

FILLING:

    2 **cups cooked dried fruit**
   ¾ **cup sugar**
    1 **teaspoon cinnamon**
   ¼ **teaspoon cloves**

Cut or chop dried fruit very fine. Add sugar and spices. Place fruit on one half of circle of dough. Fold circle in half and press edges of dough together. Pinch ends between thumb and forefinger. Bake at 375 degrees until brown, or fry in hot fat until golden brown. Delicious served hot or cold.

YIELD:
  4 to 5 servings

MEXICAN WEDDING COOKIES ❧

This delicate sweet dessert will be a surprising treat for people who think Mexican food is always hot and spicy.

  ½ **cup butter**
  2 **tablespoons confectioners' sugar**
  1 **cup flour**
  1 **cup chopped pecans**
  1 **teaspoon vanilla**

Cream together butter and sugar until light. Add flour, pecans, and vanilla. Roll dough into 1-inch balls. Place on greased baking sheet and flatten slightly. Bake at 300 degrees for 25–30 minutes. Roll in additional confectioners' sugar while warm. Let cool, roll again in sugar.

  Note: Be careful to bake only until a light brown color. Cookies may be stored for several days; sprinkle with confectioners' sugar before serving.

YIELD: 25 to 30 cookies

MARGARITA PIE ❧

  1 **14-ounce can sweetened condensed milk**
  5 **tablespoons tequila**
  5 **tablespoons triple sec**
  ½ **cup freshly squeezed lime juice**
1½ **cups whipping cream, beaten until stiff**
    graham cracker crust for 9- or 10-inch pie

Blend together condensed milk, tequila, triple sec, and lime juice. Fold in whipped cream. Pour into graham cracker crust and freeze for four hours or until firm. Serve garnished with whipped cream and a slice of lime.

ORANGE COCONUT COOKIES

Make these sweet treats ahead of time and bake when needed!

½ cup butter or margarine
½ cup light brown sugar, firmly packed
¾ cup sugar
1 egg
2 teaspoons grated orange peel
1½ teaspoons vanilla extract
1¾ cups all-purpose flour
2 teaspoons baking powder
½ teaspoon salt
½ cup flaked coconut

Soften butter; gradually add sugars and continue beating until well blended. Beat in egg, orange peel, and vanilla. Combine flour, baking powder, and salt; gradually add to creamed mixture. Blend in coconut. On a lightly floured surface form into rolls, 1½-inches in diameter. Wrap in waxed paper; chill several hours or overnight. Cut roll into ⅛-inch slices and place on un-greased baking sheets. Bake in a 400 degree oven 10 minutes, or until done. Remove to wire rack to cool.

Note: Dough may be refrigerated for one week if properly wrapped; can be frozen for up to 3 months. If frozen, thaw in refrigerator before baking.

YIELD: 6 dozen cookies

MEXICAN MOUSSE WITH ALMONDS ❧

A fantastic dessert, with delicate flavors of Mexico, easily made ahead of time.

- 4 eggs, separated
- 1 cup semi-sweet chocolate pieces
- ⅓ cup boiling water
- 3 tablespoons rum, or 2 tablespoons water and 1 teaspoon extract
- ¼ teaspoon cinnamon
- ½ teaspoon grated orange peel
- ½ cup coarsely chopped blanched almonds
- ½ cup sugar
    whipped cream
    fresh strawberries, optional

Whip egg whites until stiff. (Egg whites are easier to whip at room temperature.) In electric blender, combine chocolate pieces and boiling water; blend at medium speed until smooth. If not using blender, melt chocolate over low heat, add hot water, stir until smooth. Continue blending or mixing; add egg yolks (one at a time), rum, cinnamon, and orange peel. Gently fold whites into chocolate mixture until blended. Turn into individual dessert dishes and chill until set (overnight if possible). Meanwhile, combine almonds with sugar in heavy skillet. Stir over medium–low heat until sugar melts and turns golden. Remove from heat and pour at once onto foil or a greased cookie sheet. Cool, then break up with back of spoon.

To serve, top Mousse with a dollop of whipped cream, a sprinkle of caramelized almonds, and a fresh strawberry, if desired.

YIELD: 6 to 8 servings

MEXICAN FLAN

A popular Mexican egg custard dessert, baked in its own caramel sauce.

    8 eggs
  ⅔ cup granulated sugar
  ¼ teaspoon salt
3½ cups evaporated milk
    2 teaspoons vanilla
  ½ cup light brown sugar

Beat eggs until yolks and whites are well blended. Add granulated sugar and salt. Beat in evaporated milk and vanilla.

Sprinkle brown sugar into bottom of loaf pan; gently pour custard mixture over brown sugar. Place loaf pan in shallow baking pan containing hot water. Bake for 1 hour in 350 degree oven until knife inserted in center comes out clean. Refrigerate overnight. Before serving, run knife around edge of pan and turn out onto small platter.

To enhance this dessert's sweet flavor, after refrigerating overnight (immediately before serving) cover with thin layer of light brown sugar, place under broiler, and lightly brown.

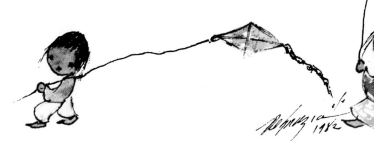

CHERRY/PEACH TORTILLA DESERT ❧

A spectacular dessert in any language. Quick and easy to make.

    1 1-pound, 5-ounce can peach or
        cherry pie filling
    4 flour tortillas
        slivered almonds
        vegetable cooking oil
        powdered sugar
        chocolate curls or semi-sweet chocolate bits

Heat tortillas by dropping into hot oil for a few seconds. Save ½ cup cherry or peach pie filling for topping. Spoon remainder onto centers of tortillas. Sprinkle 1–2 tablespoons almonds onto center of each. Fold in two sides of each tortilla and roll tortillas around filling. Heat ¼-inch oil in large skillet over medium-high heat. Place tortillas seam side down in skillet. Fry about 1 minute on each side or until light gold and crispy. Drain on paper towels to remove excess oil. Place on dessert plates. Sprinkle with powdered sugar. Top with remaining cherry or peach pie filling, some slivered almonds, and chocolate curls or semi-sweet chocolate bits. Serve hot!

YIELD: 4 servings

BEVERAGES

SANGRIA

The fruit in this wine drink is delicious to nibble from the glass. A wooden spoon makes serving easier.

- 2 oranges
- 2 lemons
- 2 fifths burgundy, or other red wine (1.5 liters)
- 8 tablespoons sugar
- 1 apple
- 1 28-ounce bottle carbonated water, chilled

Chill one orange and one lemon to be used for garnish. Squeeze juice from the second orange and lemon. Place juices, wine, burgundy, and sugar in a large pitcher or bowl. Stir to dissolve sugar; chill until time to serve. Before serving divide into two large pitchers. Cut chilled orange into wedges, slice lemon, and cut apples into slices. Divide fruit and place in pitchers of wine mixture. Stir with wooden spoon and gradually add carbonated water. Allow spoon to remain in pitcher; mix well just before serving. Serve chilled. If desired, serve over ice.

YIELD: 24 4-ounce servings

KAHLUA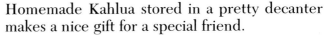

Homemade Kahlua stored in a pretty decanter makes a nice gift for a special friend.

> 3 cups water
> 3 cups sugar
> 3½ tablespoons instant coffee
> 4 teaspoons vanilla
> 1 quart vodka

Simmer together water, sugar, and coffee. Cook one hour. Cool, then add vanilla and vodka. Place in a covered container and let sit 30 days. Shake occasionally to prevent crystallization.

YIELD: Approximately 2 quarts

MEXICAN CHOCOLATE

Mexican cooks are very fond of chocolate. Even fowl and meats are cooked in spiced chocolate sauces.

> ½ cup cocoa
> 1 cup sugar
> 2½ teaspoons allspice
> 1 teaspoon cinnamon
> 2 teaspoons nutmeg
> ¼ teaspoon salt
> 1 teaspoon vanilla
> 2 quarts milk

Combine all ingredients except milk and vanilla

in 3-quart mixing bowl. Heat milk until almost boiling. Pour hot milk over dry ingredients, stirring constantly with wire whip or rotary beater. Add vanilla, mix, serve at once.

YIELD: 10 servings

PONCHE DE PIÑA

This cool, refreshing summer drink may be enhanced by a sprinkle of cinnamon frozen into the ice cubes used to chill punch.

  1 cup sugar
1½ cups water
  4 sticks cinnamon
12 cloves
  1 46-ounce can pineapple juice
1½ cups orange juice
 ½ cup lemon juice

Simmer sugar, water, cinnamon, and cloves for about 30 minutes; strain, removing cinnamon and cloves. Add pineapple, orange, and lemon juice. Pour over ice or frozen pineapple-juice cubes. One quart ginger ale may be added to serve additional guests or to give sparkly taste.

YIELD: 2 quarts

ROMPOPE

This rich cooked eggnog is also delicious made with rum. Sprinkle with ground cinnamon or nutmeg just before serving.

- 10 eggs, separated
- 4 cups milk
- ⅔ cup sugar
- 2 cinnamon sticks
- 4 tablespoons finely ground blanched almonds
- 1 cup brandy

Beat egg yolks about 5 minutes or until thick and lemon-colored. Set aside. Combine milk, sugar, and cinnamon in the top of a double boiler and bring to the boiling point, stirring frequently. Reduce heat and cook 5 minutes, stirring constantly. Remove from heat and stir gently until mixture is lukewarm. Gradually add beaten yolks and almonds. Cook once more over hot water in a double boiler until slightly thickened; allow to cool, stirring often. When liquid is cool, add brandy. Store in refrigerator for about 24 hours. Remove cinnamon stick, mix well and serve in chilled containers.

YIELD: 1 quart; 4 servings

MARGARITAS EN JARRA

Margarita, a favorite cocktail in Mexico, means daisy; beautiful when served with little daisies wound around stem of glass.

- 2 cups crushed ice
- ½ cup tequila
- ¾ cup lime juice or lemon juice
- 2 tablespoons powdered sugar
- 1 tablespoon egg white
- 1 tablespoon triple sec
- coarse salt

Combine ice, tequila, lime juice, powdered sugar, egg white, and triple sec in blender. Cover and blend until very frothy. Transfer to pitcher; garnish with slices of lime. Serve in glasses that have had rims dipped in salt.

Note: To prepare salt rim on glass, dip edge of glass first into ¼-inch lime juice, then quickly into a shallow dish of coarse salt. Shake off excess salt. Let dry at room temperature.

YIELD: 6 4-ounce servings

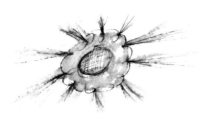

PONCHE DE CHAMPAGNE

Pineapple in bottom of punch bowl is delicious eating after punch is gone.

- 1 large fresh pineapple
- 1 tablespoon sugar
- ⅔ cup lemon juice
- 2 cups orange juice
- 1 cup light rum
- 1 pint brandy
- ½ cup orange curaçao
- 4 quarts dry champagne
- 1 orange, slice thin

Peel and slice pineapple. Reserve ½ cup, sliced into chunks, and place rest into a punch bowl. Sprinkle lightly with sugar. Add lemon juice, orange juice, rum, brandy, and curaçao. Mix to blend. Place large pieces of ice in bowl and slowly add the champagne. Stir gently. Garnish with orange slices and pineapple chunks.

YIELD: 20 to 25 servings

GLOSSARY

Albondigas: Mexican meatball soup

Burro: Large flour tortilla, warmed and filled with a variety of ingredients (usually chicken/beef, refried beans, cheese); can be served with sauce

Chili: seasoning/vegetable; green and red; generally, the smaller and more green they are, the hotter they are; used chopped, diced, whole, and dried

Chilies rellenos: stuffed green chilies

Chimichanga: type of burro; large flour tortilla folded over a meat/bean mixture and deep fried; often topped with guacamole and sour cream

Enchilada: rolled corn tortilla filled with a variety of ingredients (beans, chicken, beef) and covered with a spicy tomato-based sauce

Empanadas: Mexican turnovers, filled with a variety of fruits and sugars for dessert; with meats and sauces for a main dish

Flan: Mexican egg custard dessert, baked in caramel sauce, sometimes sprinkled with brown sugar or coffee liqueur

Flauta: rolled deep-fried corn tortilla with spicy filling

Frijoles: beans; usually pinto, often refried (cooked, mashed, and fried)

Gazpacho: a nutritious, colorful, tomato-based soup that can be served either warm or cold; will keep several days in refrigerator

Guacamole: mashed avocado, seasoned; has many uses: dip, salad, tortilla filling, garnish

Nachos: Mexican hors d'oeuvre; cheese-covered tortilla chips with zing!

Ponche: punch

Salsa: an all-purpose mixture of tomatoes and spices; used as both a dip and seasoning, as well as garnish

Sopaipillas: deep-fried squares that puff up, leaving a cavity inside that is often filled with honey

Taco: corn tortilla, fried in deep fat and bent into a U-shape, filled with a variety of ingredients: ground or shredded beef, chicken, lettuce, cheese, refried beans, etc.

Tamale: seasoned ground meat, rolled in corn meal dough, wrapped in corn husk; steamed and served with or without sauce

Tortilla: Mexican bread; made from corn meal or flour; can be stacked, rolled, folded; can be served soft, crisp, or toasted

Tostada: crisp fried corn tortilla, topped with meat, cheese, refried beans, lettuce, etc.; similar to a flat taco

INDEX

APPETIZERS